Everything Begins Elsewhere

Books by Tishani Doshi

POETRY

Everything Begins Elsewhere
Conflict and Instability (with Tobias Hill and
    Aoife Mannix)
Countries of the Body

FICTION

The Pleasure Seekers

Tishani Doshi

Everything Begins Elsewhere

Copper Canyon Press
Port Townsend, Washington

Printed in the United States of America

Cover art: Bharti Kher, *Peacock,* 2009. Bindis on painted board.
151.8 × 151.8 cm / 59¾ × 59¾ inches.

Copper Canyon Press is in residence at Fort Worden State Park
in Port Townsend, Washington, under the auspices of Centrum.
Centrum is a gathering place for artists and creative thinkers
from around the world, students of all ages and backgrounds, and
audiences seeking extraordinary cultural enrichment.

LIBRARY OF CONGRESS CATALOGING-IN-PUBLICATION DATA

Doshi, Tishani, 1975–
[Poems. Selections]
Everything begins elsewhere / Tishani Doshi.
    pages;   cm.
ISBN 978-1-55659-442-7 (pbk.: alk. paper)
I. Title.
PR9499.4.D67E95 2013
821'.92—dc23

                                                          2013009515

98765432   FIRST PRINTING

Copper Canyon Press
Post Office Box 271
Port Townsend, Washington 98368
www.coppercanyonpress.org

Chandra, again

ACKNOWLEDGMENTS

Grateful acknowledgment is made to the editors of the following publications: *Asia Literary Review, The Bloodaxe Book of Contemporary Indian Poets, The Caravan, First City, Five Dials, Guernica, The HarperCollins Book of English Poetry, Jubilee Lines: 60 Poets for 60 years, Mint, The Moth, Narrative, New Welsh Review, Poetry Review, Poetry Wales, The Rising, Sand, 60 Indian Poets, Tate Etc., Vislumbres,* and *The Warwick Review.*

"Ode to Drowning" was commissioned by Johannes Beilharz for *Inspired Poems.*

"The Dream" is forthcoming from Motionpoems.

Earlier versions of "The Dream," "Evening on an Indian Railway Platform," "Homeland," "The Immigrant's Song," "Lament—ɪ," and "Lament—ɪɪ" appeared in a chapbook, *Conflict and Instability,* commissioned by Lloyd's and Poet in the City.

Contents

Everything Begins Elsewhere

i. *Everything Begins*

Everything begins elsewhere, he knows that:
dawn, Christmas, love, beauty, terror, the wind,
the sky, the horizon, his own soul. It begins far
in the woods, or out on some windy field by the
sea. He wants to be there, not here; he wants to
be where things begin, and he is so close, he is
so *near*.

JOHN BURNSIDE, *A Lie About My Father*

Dog in the Valley

Last night
I heard a dog
in the valley
puncturing the hills
with a sound
from a long
time ago.
It was the sound
of a man and woman
falling out of love,
the sound of a century
caught in the dark.
A deep-throated howl
made under stars,
made against death,
insisting there are drums
underground,
cymbals in the clouds,
a music that goes on and on
because someone
somewhere
is listening.

Ode to Drowning

is it or is it not
the cold monsoon
bearing the shape
of my dark lord,

speaking of his cruelty,
his going away?

NAMMALVAR

I.

This is an ode
to be sung
in the latest hour of night

when rain clouds
have gathered
over shingled roofs

and blue-skinned gods
with magical flutes
seduce the virgins to dance

For there can be no love
without music
No rain

without peacocks
perched
in branches

of sandalwood trees
with plumes
of angels

and voices of thieves
pleading for their loves
to return

    II.

If rain signals
the lover's return
then I am lost

in the desert
burning
like the brainfever bird

looking for images of you
through mesquite
and teak

because there's no sign
of you
or what I know

to be as you
only clouds adrift
in a vanquished sky

like vines
of throbbing arms
and mouths

drinking at the shore
intoxicated
with the night

III.

There are as many ways
of yearning
as there are ways for rain

to fall
slow
     incessant
          gentle

squalling
        melancholy
               warm

It's that old idea
of drowning
in another to find the self

the compliance
that water gives in form
and depth

to something else
But what if the humming bees
are quiet

and the garlands of jasmine
have been laid out
to dry

How long to wait
for everything to turn
heavy with flower
        washed of dirt

IV.

It's desire after all
that spins us
Demands to be praised

as though it were new
like the stillness
before the first monsoon

when the hymen
of the earth
            is torn into

and the brazen smell
of damp
fills the air

Must there be surprise
after we've thundered
and rolled

and appeased our thirst
when the silence returns
            again

In truth
isn't it a waiting
that never ends

like the chasm between
the cycles of the world
Between separation

and union
longing and abandonment
And somewhere

between the waning
isn't this what
we're left with

the music
of uncertainty
the aftertaste of rain

Lesson 1: Building a Bridge between the Past and the Future

> The road is long. So do not mind the smallness of the present.
>
> PRAJNADEVA IN A LETTER TO
> XUANZANG, CIRCA AD 645

I. SAMSARA — THE WORLD

"Journey long," the teacher says,
so we go down, deep and deeper,
till we see ankles first, then feet.
And only after touching our heads
to the diamond back of the earth,
do we rise again, arched like curls
of river silk, emptying our souls
into the sky, forgetting the world.

II. DHAMMA — THE MEANS

We meet as lovers do, through births
and deaths, worn-down nubs of thigh
and breast, silent spaces of inadequacy.
"Come through the gates of drowning,"
the teacher says, so we cross with lotus
rafts and abandon them at the water's edge
where love's refrain is whispering: *The world
begins and then it ends. Begins and ends again.*

Xuanzang Contemplates the Wonder of Sugar on His Return Home after Sixteen Years

Here, on the roof of the world,
Xuanzang sees lights gleaming.

They could be monasteries,
or Arcadian kingdoms, or a palace

of drumbeats skirting the sands
of the great and vigilant Taklamakan.

They are something: sixteen years
and 10,000 miles away from home;

from cypress trees and hunts for treasure
in the Luo River. Xuanzang is old

and young now; keeper of the past,
bearer of the present.

He follows the bones of animals
laid out as beacons by caravans

carrying spice and indigo.
And when the dust storms rise,

wrapping their latticework of mirage
around the tamarisks,

he dreams terrible things:
of his elephant drowning,

his 657 manuscripts unfurling
like prayer flags,

scattering Sanskrit kisses
across the sky.

Was it so long ago he passed the Pamirs,
the Oxus, those mighty Bamiyan Buddhas?

When he cast himself down by the Bo tree
to weep? What was this new burning then,

spreading through the water tables
of his sandy body? Something miraculous—

those water reeds that produce honey
without bees. He reaches for it now,

deep in the folds of his travelling robes.
And it is like touching that sweetness

called childhood—a piece of nephrite jade
cradled in his river hands.

Cutting Broccoli

Between this moment and the next
there's always space for a lover's return,
though you may no longer weep for him,
or ache to lie down in the woods with him.

But say he chooses to appear on a Sunday
afternoon, when you're walking upstairs
for lunch; cutting broccoli into perfect spears
while the rice in the cooker is boiling.

Would you ask first that he strip away
the layers of the past, the times you washed
together in darkness between whispered words
and the husky calls of nightfall's birds.

Would you say how you've been waiting
for something to grow from the silence—
nothing phenomenal—just cracks of light
in the long doorways you've been walking through.

And now that he's here, do you let him
stand in the house like a newborn god,
carrying the empty weight of sky
in his eyes, saying nothing is irreversible.

Do you offer your impermanent body
against the solid frame of the kitchen door,
allow him to fall easily—into the future—
knowing the moment never disappears.

Lesson 2: Learning Mudras in Bhutan

Here, in this room of Bhutanese elders,
I learn to catch my breath again, allow my fingers
to be shaped into lotus-flower offerings
to the sky. And when I can do this 108 times without
guidance, the woman behind me—cataract-beset,
toothless, wrinkled—who's been picking stray flecks
of fleece off my back, touches me in a way you can't;
gives me the food she hasn't eaten all day, the words
she hasn't spoken. So afterwards, it is almost easy.
To walk outside where the young monks are chewing
gum in the sun, listen to them scatter down stairways
like sparrows, point to the opening of space through
which I mean to escape. I want it to be graceful,
as she was, feather touches on your jacket and a jewel
in your hands. But when the light hits us from behind
the granite cliffs, all I can muster is to lie with you
on the monastery floor, guide your fingers to the door-
ways of my weary heart, so you can feel it too—
the ocean that travels with me; how it gathers and breaks,
gathers and breaks; like love, how it stills, then parts.

Turning Off the Lights

These walls are from yesterday.

Today, rain falls like history,
and trees speak of distant woes.

My father stands on a cliff
            contemplating childhood.

By afternoon, the world has changed,
become smaller,
                  desolate.

All this is nothing—
            these red leaves on autumn walks,

these planets hurtling from long ago.

Later, we may dream of fires
                  and singing.

The house will open her doors
for the dark, salty territory of night

to enter on wet footstep,
                  falcon wing.

My father comes in to turn off the lights.

Together, he says,
        we must call in the lost,

breathe shape into all that is vanishing.

Falling, 1968

My mother arrives in India
breathless, leaning against
the airport railing, looking sad,
bereft, as though she's never put
her head against the wind before.

It is Guy Fawkes Day, 1968.
The start of National Small Pox
Eradication Week. It has been raining;
cruel, historic, monsoon rain,
uprooting posts along the border,

where Pakistan, only 21, like her,
is drowning in silver cattle skulls,
locust dreams. My father,
standing on a cusp of sudden light,
waits like sin to watch her fall.

The rest of the world is falling, too:
students, Bedouins, lorry drivers,
in West Berlin, Amman, Ootacamund.
Throwing their Marxist lives into ideas
like liberation, like love.

My mother, moving across the air
of all this, must have known how falling
in love is something like dying after all.
Something the seas and sky evade
to survive the centuries.

Perhaps this is why she agrees to tumble
to the blackened chambers of the earth
like a virgin queen ant on her nuptial flight,
burying the snow-lit nights of her youth
in galleries of dust, blades of wing.

So later, after birthing kingdoms
from the gauze of her Celtic belly,
she can say she was the illumination
once—the slow possibility
of love in my father's life.

Seasons

By October the reach of sky is complete.
Everything longs for escape—

the snow geese weaving their way south,
      the pigs in the yard,
            the leaves.

We are walking that line between the trees,
shameful in their half-foliage,
      replete with desire.

Somewhere across the valley
      there must be another life—

      a woman drawing her children a bath,
a husband returned to this picture of wife.

If we believed in seasons
      how easily we could hold to this:

this falling away and returning.

But we, who live
      with only the heat and rain,

with perpetual dying—

we, who are impervious to birdsong,

we must imagine the sound of love
        as something of a deafness—

a single vowel of longing scratched across the sky.

Evensong

after John Burnside

It's moments like this
     when the animals down by the river
are singing their lament for rain—

when fractured pieces of Canterbury
     begin to show themselves in Madras

in cloisters and coconut husks
     miracle windows of glass

It's moments like this
     I hear you on Pilgrims' Stairs

pinning the day's despair
     to the underbelly of dusk

By nightfall
     when the mosquitoes have retreated

and you've parted the skies
     for cathedral spires to rise

you'll have chanted our promise
     of togetherness
repeated it like hollows worn in stone

But it is nothing—
     this song of our communion

Less than what the animals share
       as they walk to the riverbank in slow repair

stopping to lick each other's wounds

No bonds to tie them
       to the smell of certain skin
          certain hair

That Woman

That woman is here again.
She's found her way out
from under the stairs.
For centuries she's been weeping
a song about lost men,
the disappearance of beauty,
                              disgrace.
Now she's back in the world,
down by the traffic lights,
in the shade of trees,
hurrying to the parlour
to fix the crack in her face.

Don't become that woman,
my mother said.
By which she meant,
don't become that woman
who doesn't marry
          or bear children.
That woman who spreads her legs,
who is beaten, who cannot hold
her grief or her drink.
Don't become that woman.

But that woman and I
have been moving together
              for years,
like a pair of birds
skimming the water's surface,
always close to the soft

madness of coming undone;
the dark undersides of our bodies
       indistinguishable
from our reflections.

Lesson 3: Stillness

All morning I try to hold it—
the desperation of a fly
beating against glass,
a dog's distant bark,
the dull throb of a lorry
winding its way up the hills.

By afternoon I think I've mastered it.
Nothing the world offers me
can be as complete or as full as this.
When I step into the light,
I have no song for the stones,
no thought for the grass.

I only want to remember
this long road,
this steady pulse,
which feels like love.
So when evening
feeds itself to night,
clearing the way
for frost or flood,

I'll still be left with this—
the bright suffocation of flowers,
the weight of the day's hours.

The River of Girls

i.m. India's missing girls

This is not really myth or secret.
This murmur in the mouth
of the mountain where the sound
of rain is born. This surging
past pilgrim town and village well.
This coin-thin vagina
and acid stain of bone.
This doctor with his rusty tools,
this street cleaner, this mother
laying down the bloody offerings
of birth. This is not the cry
of a beginning, or a river
buried in the bowels of the earth.
This is the sound of ten million girls
singing of a time in the universe
when they were born with tigers
breathing between their thighs;
when they set out for battle
with all three eyes on fire,
their golden breasts held high
like weapons to the sky.

Ode to the Walking Woman

after Alberto Giacometti

Sit—
you must be tired
of losing yourself
this way:
a bronzed rib
of exhaustion
thinned out
against the night.
Sit—
there are still things
to believe in
like civilizations
and birthing
and love.
And ancestors
who move
like silent tributaries
from red-earthed villages
with history cradled
in their mythical arms.
But listen,
what if they swell
through the gates
of your glistening city?
Will you walk down
to the water's edge,
immerse your feet
till you can feel them
dancing underneath?
Mohenjo Daro's brassy girls

with bangled wrists
and cinnabar lips;
turbaned Harappan mothers
standing wide
on terra-cotta legs;
egg-breasted Artemis—
Inanna, Ishtar, Cybele,
clutching their bounteous hearts
in the unrepentant dark,
crying: *Daughter,*
why have the granaries
and great baths disappeared?
Won't you resurrect yourself,
make love to the sky,
reclaim the world?

Another Man's Woman

My lover has failed to come to the trysting place,
It is perhaps that his mind is dazed, or perhaps
that he went to another woman,
Or lured perhaps by festive folk, that he delays,
Or perhaps along the dark fringe of the forest he
wanders lost.

JAYADEVA

If we lived in another age,
I'd have been the kind of woman
who refused to cast down her eyes.
The kind of woman
the other maids in town despise
because she forgets to tie up the calves
and split the curds.
You know the kind—
with a tilt in her hips
and hair that slips
continually
from her braids.

But since we live in a world
that's just reflection,
perhaps I can be her after all—
the one whose hips defeat the mountains
with their greatness,
whose breasts are heavy,
close, and high—
            sandal-pasted;
who walks through moonless nights
with lotus skin and lotus feet
across forbidden boundaries.

I'll be the kind who sallies out
to wait for love
with musk-kissed hair
and navel bared
in a thousand secret places—
past the cowsheds
and the balsam grove,
across the river,
in the garden of hibiscus.

And although the night be dark
and fierce enough to stir
the seven sleeping oceans, I'll deceive the forest
like a shadow,
slip noiselessly past
evil eyes and serpent tongues
and the husband who lies inside
jealous of my devotion.

But if I should reach the riverbank
and see you there—
combing another woman's hair.
If I should see the girdle
loosen from her waist
while you string jasmine
round her supine face.
If you should drink the honeyed sweet
from the petals
of her crimsoned lips—

I won't question this betrayal,
or ask who this other woman is.

I'll simply walk
into the dark
where every trunk
and branch and leaf
looks like you, feels like you,
speaks like you: deep-chested
                    yellow-limbed
                              rain-cloud blue.

And later, while the husband sleeps,
I'll make my way
to the town's cremation grounds.
I'll strip away my clothes
and dance among the mounds of ash
to command the churning of a storm.
For I have been with you
since you were born,
and will stay with you
till you return,
soaked with the lasting dawn.

ii. *Elsewhere*

"Journeys to relive your past?" was the Khan's question at this point, a question which could also have been formulated: "Journeys to recover your future?"

And Marco's answer was: "Elsewhere is a negative mirror. The traveler recognizes the little that is his, discovering the much he has not had and will never have."

ITALO CALVINO, Invisible Cities

Buffaloes

Impossible to imagine.
Buffaloes—a dream of them:
coats thick with rain,
bodies like continents.
A whole world thundering
through Indian laburnum.
Think of beginnings:
amusement parks at dawn,
pianos, bedrooms, gods.
Think of all the invisible
insurrections it takes
to wake a city from slumber.
In these woods, a single man
will do, armed with a stick
and a paltry collection of stones.
When I see buffaloes run
I think of love—how it is held
in the meaty, muscled pink
of the tongue; how quickly
it is beaten from us—
all that brute resolve
            disappearing
in the undergrowth.

Michael Mangal's Dream

The nights grow long in Pillowpanja
      with all the people gone,

thinks Michael Mangal,
      lying insect-style on his back

where his house used to be.

      The stars seem closer too—
bare-boned, full of promises,

in this month-old lacerated sky
      abandoned by the gods.

He could lie like this—
      waiting for the winds to change,

for a spirit's gentle finger to turn him over.

Or he could dream of pigs in pandanus
      from Christmas lunch;

of the woman from next door
      whom he never told he loved,

to reappear from the Kingdom of the Sea
      and save him.

        ∽

At daybreak he will scour the beach,
        sift through broken bamboo stilts

       and ravaged roofs,
a million orphaned carcasses.

He will lean against the ocean floor,
       and imagine
            the woman from next door

is offering up her watery chest
       so he can listen for the sounds

of all the friends he's feasted with,
         built precarious houses with.

And later, when they finally speak of love,
        she can drag him with her spirit hands

to that underworld of longing
       and deliverance

where the season of the rains begins—

       where children
saved inside their fathers' thighs,

with gleaming backs
       and startled eyes,
learn to walk the sands again.

After the Rains

After the rains
the temple flowers
lie like fallen soldiers—
dirtied and bloodied pink.
I want to get down
on bended knee,
gather each broken petal
to my chest.
Out there—
where the river meets
the ocean's mouth—
it would be called
the kiss of life,
a resuscitation.
But here,
with the world washed clean,
it is nothing but a trampling.

Found Poem

Diane Ackerman, *A Natural History of the Senses*

One night a year,
in the Bahamas,
the *Selenicereus* cactus flowers
ache
into bloom,
conduct their entire sex lives,
and vanish by morning.

Fisher-Price Men

I'd forgotten about them,
those thumb-sized men
who lived for years
on our bedroom floor.
They were my brother's treasures:
the green Texan, the road builders,
the circus ringmaster—
all hatted and moustachioed,
tunnelling out of the past
bearing the scars
of our dead dog's tooth-marks.

Today, my sister's boy from America
brings the village alive again,
leading the men to camper vans
and dusty deckchairs,
giving them names
like Harvey and Stan.
My brother sits in the corner,
rocking, oblivious.
He doesn't rise to greet his childhood
spread out on the bedroom floor,
or say, *Mine, all mine*,
as he used to.
He is in a place of no time,
with no thoughts of death or fear.
Only the sound
of his beating heart,
which must tell him
that he is human,
that he too is moving somewhere.

Lesson 4: Zero, or Infinity (Ramanujan)

The man who knew infinity was born
not far from me, in December,
a long time ago.
It is December now.
The sky cranes her neck
towards the Sunday streets.
The universe does nothing
to steer this loneliness away.
Night brings the moon,
barbs and wings,
a thousand scatterings.
There's a place that poets seek
as real and fearsome as the body.
When I find this place
I will lie down in it,
the dark, pockmarked endlessness of it.
The man who knew infinity
will be there, too,
unravelling the mysteries of zero.
He knows what it means
to take away, yet keep things whole,
to give without diminishing.
It is December now.
The poets fill rooms with dust,
and we still know nothing of love.
When I say, *Come,*
only the sky leaks in,
and stays a while.

Evening on an Indian Railway Platform

This is the time when ragpickers appear
with sun-bleached hair and hollowed chests,
when vendors replenish their wooden carts,
when stray dogs steal across railway tracks
with blood on their paws and the wind
on their backs, when televisions splutter
through cyclones and genocides,
when families in waiting rooms empty
tiffin carriers onto newspaper squares
to fill their bellies with rice, and stare.

After days of silence, we have arrived.
We will stretch our bodies along beds
that fold into walls, and dream our way back
to a city where dust storms into the house
with flies. Later, I will leave you, knotted
in a ball of sleep. But for now, I am
like one of those ragpickers—sun-bleached,
unseen. I lift up my skirt to squat
over a tin hole in the ground, and it feels
as though I'm squatting over the universe,
raining down on it like a queen.

The Dream

The dream has always been simple—
    a porch so the old folks
        can sit out in summer,

a garden for vegetables,
        children, pets,
a picket fence to keep them in.

The dream has always been about safety.

So even as we sit alone
    in our high-rise buildings
and basement apartments

where the outside world comes
    to sit at our windows
        like a tattered, yellow thing,

the dream is always
    on the horizon—
        glittering.

The Adulterous Citizen

> I am an adulterous resident; when I am in
> one city, I am dreaming of the other. I am an
> exile; citizen of the country of longing.
>
> SUKETU MEHTA, *Maximum City*

When it comes to it,
there's only the long, paved road
that leads to a house
with a burning light.
A house you can never own,
but allows you
to sleep in its bed
without demanding sex,
eat from its cupboards
without paying,
lie in the granite cool of its tub
without drowning.
And only when the first shards
of day slice through
the blinds
of the basement windows,
nudging you
with something of a whisper—
something like, *Maybe it's time to go*—
do you finally drag
your suitcases
up the carpeted stairs,
out the front door,
on to the summer pavements.

It is nothing
like losing a lover,
or leaving behind

the lanes of childhood.
Nothing like scaling
the winged walls of memory
to discover your friends
have packed up their boxes
and vanished.
More like stumbling
into a scene from the future,
where the ghost
of a husband
beckons with pictures
of a family
you no longer recognise,
and other people's children
race across the grass,
lulling you into belief
that you can always return like this—
without key in hand,
to lie in the folds of one city,
while listening to the jagged,
carnal breaths of another.

The Immigrant's Song

Let us not speak of those days
when coffee beans filled the morning
with hope, when our mothers' headscarves
hung like white flags on washing lines.
Let us not speak of the long arms of sky
that used to cradle us at dusk.
And the baobabs—let us not trace
the shape of their leaves in our dreams,
or yearn for the noise of those nameless birds
that sang and died in the church's eaves.
Let us not speak of men,
stolen from their beds at night.
Let us not say the word
                    disappeared.
Let us not remember the first smell of rain.
Instead, let us speak of our lives now—
the gates and bridges and stores.
And when we break bread
in cafés and at kitchen tables
with our new brothers,
let us not burden them with stories
of war or abandonment.
Let us not name our old friends
who are unravelling like fairy tales
in the forests of the dead.
Naming them will not bring them back.
Let us stay here, and wait for the future
to arrive, for grandchildren to speak
in forked tongues about the country
we once came from.
Tell us about it, they might ask.

And you might consider telling them
of the sky and the coffee beans,
the small white houses and dusty streets.
You might set your memory afloat
like a paper boat down a river.
You might pray that the paper
whispers your story to the water,
that the water sings it to the trees,
that the trees howl and howl
it to the leaves. If you keep still
and do not speak, you might hear
your whole life fill the world
until the wind is the only word.

Madras Morning

It is early in Madras
and the temple priests are busy
with their morning prayers
like the walkers and the joggers
and the coffee makers at Hi-Cool
and Re-Lax and Maheshwari Snacks
and the bus drivers and taxi drivers
who've left their dreams in bed
and the vegetable sellers
and the call-centre boys and girls
who are practising their accents
on their way to work
and the construction workers
with thermometer-shaped legs
and the air hostesses in green
comparing heels
and the stewards and the clerks
in brass-buttoned coats
and the Air India pilots
sneaking their last smoke
and we who've kissed
the children goodbye
and left instructions
with the maid
we who don't know
how easily the world
moves without us
we are sitting upright in chairs
balancing trays on our knees
eating the air

Lesson 5: Saying Goodbye to Love in Butoh Class

To begin we are one-celled creatures—
blind, wildly incompetent, pawing about
in the waters of the dark. Then we grow
spines, limbs, feel the ghost movement
in our coccyges—the memory of tails.
There is such a thing as tiger life—
a primitive pattern of the universe
imprinted in our hearts. We may walk
with lotus flowers in our palms,
a forest of cherry blossoms bursting
from our heads, shoulders, arms,
but sooner or later we will have to know
the earth, to understand *bereft*.
Sooner or later, we will have to confront
the charred corpse of a cedar tree,
an orphaned child, a friend in the rubble
dying slowly, terribly. What should we say?
How should we mend these fissures
of loss when the wind howls so,
when we can hear death coming for us?
Learn to embrace the past. Yes, learn
to embrace. But when the past arrives,
cloaked with forgotten smells, the smooth,
musky assault of it on our bodies,
all I see is love—another and another,
            carrying his own elixir
of   ocean   oil   bone.
I fix my gaze, breathe—let go—breathe.
They come wearing bells. They will not leave
until it is winter, and they are kissed free.

Lines to a Lover from a Previous Century

after Mir

My love, I have grown old waiting.
My body is no longer tall
        or graceful as the cypress.
When I walk it is no longer
as if spring were approaching.
My hips don't sway as they used to,
like flower-laden branches
moving in the morning breeze.
The coral of my lips,
        the pearl of my cheeks,
            the raven tresses of my hair—
they have been ravaged by time
and no longer know how
to ensnare a young man's heart,
or intoxicate like wine.

I have been waiting so long, my love,
for you to take me in your arms
as gently as night envelops evening
            to its breast.
I have kept vigil by this window,
waiting for your shadow to grow
from the west, for the sound of your step,
for the sweet lilt of your voice from afar.
Are you not tired of being away, dear heart?
Do you not long to hold me one last time
so we can leave this world
with our bodies as bright as the moon
            and stars?

I have grown old waiting, my love,
and this is not a country for the aged.
The lovers here know nothing of time,
                of how the soul must pine
before there can be togetherness again.
These women do not blush at a man's gaze.
Nothing tears their hearts. Nothing breaks.
And the men, they don't understand longing,
                or the thousand yearnings of the heart.
They only want to hold the moment.
Now, they say. Now, as if it were everything.
Now, they want to see and talk and touch.
And when these men leave behind their beloveds,
they are not like moths to the flame.
They do not wander the lanes, lost,
speaking aloud their lovers' names.

My love, it has been years since you were here,
but my eyes still see you every day, my heart
                still beats for your touch.
If you would come to the garden one last time
to pass the long night in my arms,
I promise not to hide when morning comes,
but to see you off into the fields,
to wander there on blistered feet.
Because *I knew that love would take my life as forfeit.*
When I began I knew how I would end.
Just come to me once again,
so when it's time to meet my maker
I'll know to ask the breeze
where to find the vagabond of love.
And when the breeze gathers up
a little dust into the air,
my love, I'll know to end this wait,
                and follow it like a prayer.

The Magic of the Foot

Think of the magic of that foot,
comparatively small, upon which your
whole weight rests. It's a miracle, and
the dance is a celebration of that miracle.

MARTHA GRAHAM

After
when your body
no longer belongs to you
when it's still out there
in last night's darkness
seeking its way
into the sublime
those tendril feet
licking against the spine
of the stage,
After the lights
and the thrum of applause
have lifted into the streets
and slipped
into strangers' apartments
to live between wall hangings
and philosophy books
like remnants,
After all this
don't be surprised
to find yourself
in the same position again
splayed out on the bedroom floor
legs prised open
like a jewel box
the hinges
singing odes to joy

and the feet
those tiny miracles
pushing up and around
until they are joined
like hands
meeting wildly
unforgettably.

Love Poem

Ultimately, we will lose each other
to something. I would hope for grand
circumstance—death or disaster.
But it might not be that way at all.
It might be that you walk out
one morning after making love
to buy cigarettes, and never return,
or I fall in love with another man.
It might be a slow drift into indifference.
Either way, we'll have to learn
to bear the weight of the eventuality
that we will lose each other to something.
So why not begin now, while your head
rests like a perfect moon in my lap,
and the dogs on the beach are howling?
Why not reach for the seam in this South Indian
night and tear it, just a little, so the falling
can begin? Because later, when we cross
each other on the streets, and are forced
to look away, when we've thrown
the disregarded pieces of our togetherness
into bedroom drawers and the smell
of our bodies is disappearing like the sweet
decay of lilies—what will we call it,
when it's no longer love?

Lesson 6: How Not to Age

It happens one night that the hurdles champ
of Loyola, Class of '58, finds himself on the lawns
of a gentlemen's club—shoulders stooped,
bandy-kneed, unable to hear or digest sugar.
It happens his wife dies first, and his children
frequently think, *hypothetically,* if Dad had gone
first, Mum would still have had things to do.
It happens that the man who threw the best parties,
the first person in town with disco lights,
psychedelic shirts, the works—now finds it difficult
to smile. And as if to prove this unhappy man
once had the capacity to dance, the moon skids over
his spectacles, does a little jig on the wintry expanse
of his head, eclipsing for a moment this night,
these stars, all the borrowed future ahead.

Lament —1

When I see the houses in this city,
the electric gates and uniformed men
employed to guard the riches of the rich,
the gilded columns and gardens,
the boats on water, I wonder,
how to describe my home to you:
the short, mud walls,
the whispering roof, the veranda
on which my whole family
used to spread sheets and sleep.

The year I came to find work in the city,
my wife painted our house white
so it would be brighter than the neighbours'.
I beat her for her foolishness.
The children are hungry, I said,
the cow is old,
the money collector is after my blood,
and you steal like a magpie—
half a month's wage—to decorate
your nest like a shiny jewel?

The monsoon finally arrived the year I left,
dripped through the thatch,
peeled paint off the walls.
The wells grew full and overflowed.
The farmers rejoiced in the fields.
My son sat with his mouth open
catching drops of water like a frog.
My wife clung to the walls and wept.

When I fall asleep on the pavements
in this city, I try to imagine my wife's skin
against mine, the kohl in her eyes,
the white walls, the whole village sky
bearing down upon us
with all the weight of the stars.
I think of returning to that life,
but mostly I try to remember
how the world was once.
I want to open my mouth like my son,
and swallow things whole—
feel water filling all the voids,
until I am shaped back into existence.

By morning she has lost
a husband, a home, a dream,
a night of her life
that will never return.
She tries not to think
of what she will do,
of what this means
in the long history of loss.
There are tigers dying,
she knows, nuclear threats
that might eradicate
the world.
Forests are disappearing,
and seas are being emptied.
She tries not to think
of her hunger
against the magnitude of all this.
Her small hunger against
the failure of civilizations.
She thinks instead
of evening,
how once again
it will grow long and bright,
how eternity that seemed
so paltry just minutes ago
could become eternal once again.
She thinks of the moon
rising in the cleft of the distant hills.
It is the only comfort

she allows herself—
to relinquish the things she loves
as if they were never hers.

Walking Around

after Neruda

It happens that I am tired of being a woman.
It happens that I cannot walk past country clubs
or consulates without considering the hags,
skinny as guitar strings, foraging in the rubbish.

All along the streets there are forlorn mansions
where girls have grown up and vanished.
I am vanishing, too. I want nothing to do with gates
or balconies or flat-screen TVs.

It happens that I am tired of my veins and my hips,
and my navel and my sorrows.
It happens that I am tired of being a woman.

Just the same it would be joyous
to flash my legs at the watchmen playing chess,
to lead the old man at house 38
onto the tarred road to lie down
under the laburnum dripping gold.

I do not want to keep growing in this skin,
to swell to the size of a mausoleum.
I do not want to be matriarch or mother.
Understand, I am in love
with only these undrunk breasts.

And when Monday arrives with the usual
battalion of pear-shaped wives who do battle
in grocery store aisles,

I'll be stalking the fields of concrete and ash,
the days pushing me from street
to street, leading me elsewhere—
to houses without ceiling fans
where daughters disappear and the walls weep.

I will weep too for high-heeled beauty queens,
for sewing machines and chickens in cages.
I will walk with my harness
and exiled feet through cravings
and renunciations, through heaps
of midnight wreckages
where magistrates of crows gather
to sing the same broken song
of unforgiving loss.

Lesson 7: How to Dream a Beautiful Death

In the dream of his death
Rinpoche returns to the room
of his youth—the wood beams,
the barking dogs, the fields
of potato and wheat; mother
with her prayer beads
by the window grilles,
muttering grace after grace;
sister in the kitchen
preparing flasks of tea.

In the dream of his death
Rinpoche sits in a fur-lined coat
hemmed into the window light,
waiting for father to come home
and hold him. *Gone, gone,*
he says, *gone altogether beyond.*
Because this is how he wants to go—
like an ochre flower in a field,
hungry and alive, the wind rushing in,
scattering him everywhere.

This is how it could be
in our own dreams of dying.
If we believed in mandalas, those maps
that guide us from periphery
to centre, and over to the other shore,
we'd know we're always where
we're meant to be—lying down

among the trees, covered in coats
of bark and mud, waiting for the sages
to lead us out of the forests, to the sea.

Homeland

What if the dead came back as bandits—
        a whole army of them on herds of camels,
brandishing swords and Kalashnikovs?

What if they could reclaim our land
        with weapons instead of words?

If they came to our roofless shelters
        at night with salves for our wounds
           and water for our lips?

If the dead could speak,
        would they ask for us:
           brother, child, wife.

Would they be able to mend
        the rape's scar,
breathe life into these corroded fields?

If they could lie down
        on this dust-choked earth
           to hold us,

would they trace
        the wooden shafts of our bones,

dismantle the starlit domes
     of these desert nights,

whisper, *Love, sweet love,*
     it is I. I am home.

Memory of Wales

This is how it arrives, the memory
of Wales, on a day of scanty light.
I'm walking towards the playground.
I will never know newness like this,
or fear. I'm walking, and I'm eight.
I see a girl on the swing—my mother,

or at least, a version of my mother:
fair-haired, small. In the memory
of Wales it is often cold. I'm eight
and the cows are stalking light
like monsters in the playground.
I will never know newness like this.

I will never know a world like this.
This is my childhood and my mother's.
Everything begins in the playground:
beauty, decay, love, lilies. Memory
starts here on the stairs, in skylight.
Cows chew eternally. I'm eight

in this memory, I'm always eight.
There's a painting that speaks to this
malady of recurrence—an indigo twilight
of melting clocks, which shows Mother
Time as a kind of persistence, memory
and dream, coupling on the ground.

Everything we love returns to the ground.
Mother, father, childhood. When I'm eight
I know nothing of betrayal, but the memory
persists. Only once, is it different from this.
The playground is empty, and my mother,
no longer a girl, is walking a ridge of light.

Now she's at the wooden gate. Light
from Welsh stars tumbles to the ground.
Bronze cliffs in the distance sing. My mother
has met a man. She's going away. I'm eight,
but I've always known she'll leave all this.
Forsaking, after all, is a kind of memory.

My mother is eight and in Wales again.
She's in the playground of memory,
swinging towards light, towards this.

The Art of Losing

It begins with the death
of the childhood pet—
the dog who refuses to eat
for days, the bird or fish
found sideways, dead.
And you think the hole
in the universe,
caused by the emission
of your grief, is so deep
it will never be rectified.
But it's only the start
of an endless litany
of betrayals:
the cruelty of school,
your first bastard boyfriend,
the neighbour's son
going slowly mad.
You catch hold of losing,
and suddenly, it's everywhere—
the beggars in the street,
the ravage of a distant war
in your sleep.
And when grandfather
hobbles up to the commode
to relieve himself like a girl
without bothering to shut
the door, you begin to realise
what it means to exist
in a world without.
People around you grow old

and die, and it's explained
as a kind of going away—
to God, or rot, or to return
as an ant. And once again,
you're expected to be calm
about the fact that you'll never see
the dead again,
never hear them enter a room
or leave it,
never have them touch
the soft parting of your hair.
Let it be, your parents advise:
it's nothing.
Wait till your favourite aunt
keels over in a shopping mall,
or the only boy you loved
drives off a cliff and survives,
but will never walk again.
That'll *really* do you in,
make you want to slit your wrists
(in a metaphorical way, of course,
because you're strong and know
that life is about surviving these things).
And almost all of it might
be bearable if it would just end
at this. But one day your parents
will sneak into the garden
to stand under the stars,
and fade, like the lawn,
into a mossy kind of grey.
And you must let them.
Not just that.
You must let them pass
into that wilderness
and understand that soon,

you'll be called aside
to put away your paper wings,
to fall into that same oblivion
with nothing.
As if it was nothing.

Visiting My Parents in Summer

It seems they have always been here—
these crows outside the window,
whom I cannot see, but hear.
It seems they have been making their noise
for such a long time I can no longer remember
what it was like before.
Perhaps it was summer
and there were leaves on the ground
from trees silently dying.
Perhaps it is still summer
and all you are doing is listening
to your life pass by
in a single afternoon.
Here is your childhood room.
Here are the distances between sleeps.
And here are the crows outside the window
singing their harsh song, glistening.

Love Poem Disguised as an Elegy

When I see you these days
you are always at a party,
standing by a window, alone,
growing younger and younger.
Heaven's great, you say.
You and Saddam are pals,
and from this distance,
everything is forgiven.
Do you remember when...
But never mind.
It's always that last picture:
you propped up in bed,
your legs slightly raised,
the smell of piss,
purple sores,
a rebel body in disrepair.
Hush, you say, I have to go,
but remember, the heart
isn't a muscle, it isn't even a thing
that beats. It's what you love.
It's what you're doing today.

There'll be a time you grow
so young you won't know me,
and this is terrifying
because I still have things to ask
about the body and dying
and where memories go to live.
Just once, I'd like to see you
with the flower girls

back at the gate.
It wouldn't matter then,
if nothing like you
ever happened to me again.
It would have been enough
to have seen you change
into something small and golden,
charging off into the waves
on your strong, white legs.
What need would there be
to speak of danger,
after you were gone, vanished,
like a dream into the day.

for Chandralekha, who died on 30 December 2006, the
same day that Saddam Hussein was executed, also the
auspicious Hindu day of Vaikuntha Ekadashi, when the
gates of heaven are supposedly open to all

After the Dance

i.m. Chandralekha
(1928–2006)

After the dance I imagine you
resurrected into this uncertain world.
It is midnight and the moon hovers
close to the trees, who are your daughters
and sons, planted in this desert
so many moons ago. After the dance
the audience drifts like dinner guests,
drowsy and replete. Those who knew you,
who are still filled with astonishment,
stand at the gate and say, *She was everywhere.*
Only later, when the theatre empties
and morning creeps into the dark,
when something of the day's vituperous
heat makes its way down from the stars,
do I see you sitting in your favourite chair,
batting flies off your lips,
smoothening down your silver hair.

About the Author

Tishani Doshi was born in Madras, India, in 1975. She received her masters in writing from Johns Hopkins University and worked in London in advertising before returning to India in 2001. At the age of twenty-six, an encounter with the legendary choreographer Chandralekha led her to an unexpected career in dance. In 2006, her book of poems *Countries of the Body* won the Forward Poetry Prize for best first collection in the UK. She is also the recipient of an Eric Gregory Award for poetry and winner of the All-India Poetry Competition. Her first novel, *The Pleasure Seekers,* was published to critical acclaim in 2010 and has been translated into several languages. It was long-listed for the Orange Prize and the International IMPAC Dublin Literary Award and short-listed for the Hindu Literary Prize. Doshi now divides her time between a village by the sea in South India, and elsewhere.

Poetry is vital to language and living. Since 1972, Copper Canyon Press has published extraordinary poetry from around the world to engage the imaginations and intellects of readers, writers, booksellers, librarians, teachers, students, and donors.

WE ARE GRATEFUL FOR THE MAJOR SUPPORT PROVIDED BY:

THE PAUL G. ALLEN
FAMILY FOUNDATION

Lannan

THE MAURER FAMILY
FOUNDATION

NATIONAL
ENDOWMENT
FOR THE ARTS

WASHINGTON STATE
ARTS COMMISSION

Anonymous

Arcadia Fund

John Branch

Diana and Jay Broze

Beroz Ferrell & The Point, LLC

Mimi Gardner Gates

Gull Industries, Inc.
on behalf of William and Ruth True

Mark Hamilton and Suzie Rapp

Carolyn and Robert Hedin

Steven Myron Holl

Rhoady and Jeanne Marie Lee

Maureen Lee and Mark Busto

Brice Marden

New Mexico Community Foundation

H. Stewart Parker

Penny and Jerry Peabody

Joseph C. Roberts

Cynthia Lovelace Sears and Frank Buxton

The Seattle Foundation

Dan Waggoner

Charles and Barbara Wright

The dedicated interns and faithful
volunteers of Copper Canyon Press

To learn more about underwriting Copper Canyon Press titles,
please call 360-385-4925 ext. 103

The Chinese character for poetry is made up of two parts: "word" and "temple." It also serves as pressmark for Copper Canyon Press.

The text is set in Aldus, designed by Hermann Zapf, with titles set in FB Californian, a digital version of Frederic Goudy's typeface California. Book design and composition by VJB/Scribe. Printed on archival-quality paper by McNaughton & Gunn, Inc.